GEORG KAISER

GAS I

A Play in Five Acts

Introduction by
VICTOR LANGE
Princeton University

FREDERICK UNGAR PUBLISHING CO.
NEW YORK

Published by arrangement with
Mrs. Margaret Kaiser

Translated by Herman Scheffauer

Eighth Printing, 1980

Copyright ©1957, 1963 by
Frederick Ungar Publishing Co., Inc.

Printed in the United States of America

ISBN 0-8044-6343-3
Library of Congress Catalog Card No. 63-22147

INTRODUCTION

THE CHANGES in feeling and perception that began to take shape among the poets and painters at the turn of this century, culminating in the revolutionary drama of German expressionism, can hardly be more effectively illustrated than by Georg Kaiser's *Gas*. Uncompromising in its break with the dramaturgical conventions of the psychological play that had reached its perfection in the achievements of Ibsen, Kaiser's work is cast in a form carefully calculated to convey a modern issue: it is concerned not with the alternatives of individual behavior but with the collective experience of a moral crisis brought about by the consequences of contemporary economic and technological practices.

It is not surprising that this theme should have been stated most bluntly by the German writers of the early twenties. A once vigorous and self-confident society found itself disintegrating in the wake of the defeat of 1918; and the subsequent turmoil of political upheaval and economic collapse created the climate for desperate outbursts of imaginative energy. Much of that expressionist literature is utopian: it devoted itself to a scrutiny of those human resources that might help in the rebuilding of what had been destroyed, and it turned fervently and even angrily to an analysis of those forces that seemed most inimical to a better life. But where it advanced beyond a bitter denunciation of the past, it proclaimed an image of the human being which, naive and unduly idealistic though it may seem, yet projected an order of society in which sentient and compassionate man was to be the master and not the victim of his own aspirations.

It is clear that so intense and radical a vision should excite,

1

above all, the sensibilities of the lyrical poets, in whose work the double cry of accusation and hope can be heard again and again. But where the revolutionary message is proclaimed not merely with fervor and faith but as a challenge to be dialectically argued, it produced a curiously persuasive type of theatre. In the plays of some of these authors, lyricism and ideological convictions are often intermingled; others are less sentimental but aggressively critical of middle-class beliefs; only Georg Kaiser, an immensely productive and versatile playwright, succeeded in maintaining an artistic balance between the passion of the social revolutionary, an incorruptible eye for the logic inherent in an intellectual proposition, and the technical skill of an expert in theatre.

Georg Kaiser was born in Magdeburg, Germany, in 1878. As the son of a well-to-do merchant his business career seemed assured: he was sent to Argentina to work for one of the largest German power concerns, but, after three years in Buenos Aires, his health failing, he returned to Europe and lived in Italy and Spain before settling in the vicinity of Berlin. During the twenties he was the most productive of the German playwrights, and in 1930 was elected to the German Academy—a distinction of which the Nazi government deprived him four years later. Being in his social views sharply in conflict with the prevailing political climate in Germany, he emigrated to Switzerland. He continued to produce plays, fiction, and poetry. Much of this later work is not yet available in print; but it is clear that the work of his last fifteen years differs in many respects from those plays that established his reputation as an "expressionist" writer. He died in Ascona in 1945.

Kaiser's career is not easily summarized, nor has his total achievement yet received adequate critical treatment. In more than seventy plays—thirteen of them produced in 1917-18 alone —ranging from brittle comedies to savage attacks upon the delusions of his age, from modern farces to sustained tragedies in the Greek manner, he deals again and again with the forces of unreason and delusion that threaten contemporary man. Kaiser is first and foremost a moralist: his theme is the "renewal of man,"

2

the search for those authentic qualities in the human being that will prove durable and creative beyond the paralysis of judgment.

Like Gerhart Hauptmann, whom alone he rivals in popularity, Kaiser is a social dramatist without doctrinaire convictions; but, different from Hauptmann, he limits the scope and mobility of the individual and subjects it to the inexorable logic of circumstance and technical realities. In one of his early plays, *From Morn Till Midnight* (1916), Kaiser examines, in a series of high-pitched scenes, the pathetic efforts of a bank teller who breaks out of his routine existence to find meaning and integrity. No familiar form of social life can provide it for him: he can in the end assert it only for himself. He dies a martyr in a sacrificial act of self-destruction.

Gas (1917-20) is a dramatic project of greater scope and intensity. It consists of three plays, *Die Koralle, Gas I,* and *Gas II*.

In *Die Koralle* (The Coral), the first play of this trilogy, the theme of integrity—the utopian theme of the "new man"—is elaborated in the context of an individual life: the millionaire (or, as Kaiser with characteristic overemphasis calls him, the "billionaire") seeks in vain to cast off the haunting shadow of an unhappy childhood; he murders his double in order to obtain not only happiness but identity.

Gas I (1918), the second play of the trilogy, advances the argument from a private issue to a group experience. In *The Coral* the billionaire's son had chosen a life of rebellion against injustice and exploitation. He now becomes a social revolutionary dedicated to a realization of the "new man." He offers his workers the opportunity of a humane life; but the reforms he proposes and the prospect of an equal share in profits lead only to an intensification of greed among the workers and to their total dependence upon the machines. They will not abandon the production of a highly lucrative but dangerous gas upon which the huge machinery of capitalism depends but which threatens from time to time to destroy the plant and the workers. After a disastrous explosion which, as Kaiser puts it, seems to have been "dictated from beyond," the workers demand

3

the dismissal of the engineer. The billionaire's son intervenes: not the explosion, he insists, but the inescapable tyranny of the machine threatens their lives. He proposes a utopian community on the grounds of the wrecked factory in which the workers may lead a creative life. The engineer's persuasive opposition, and the prospects of fat government contracts defeat this scheme. At the cost of their happiness the workers prefer the "system" to "life": the new man is not yet. The billionaire's son is resigned, his vision of a humane life has come to naught, his hopes for the future seem beyond realization.

For in *Gas II* (1920) the world is engulfed in apocalyptic destruction: the impact of fanatical technological thinking upon the human being is demonstrated most dramatically. The great-grandson of the billionaire is now one of the workers in a state-run plant; in an effort at preventing imminent total war he proclaims the ideals of meekness and brotherly love instead of self-ambition and battle. He fails. Not victory but the radical destruction of both warring sides is the inescapable result. The voice of the visionary cries in a wilderness of inhumanity: beyond the evidence of barbarism he can only project a dream of peace in another world.

The three plays, each artistically and intellectually complete in itself, may at first sight seem profoundly skeptical of the very idealism that constituted the chief impulse of the German expressionist poet. Yet they provide in fact the poetic elaboration, in extreme images and situations, of the economic and social implications of capitalism as Kaiser and the German revolutionary intelligentsia saw them after the First World War. The exploitational character of money and the concomitant paralysis of the individual leaves the billionaire in *The Coral* with only the essentially romantic desire for self-extinction; in *Gas I* his son proclaims an ethical socialism which is doomed to failure in the face of collective blindness and the compelling or persuasive interests of the state; in *Gas II* state socialism itself leads to a holocaust in which the "blue figures" of capitalism and the "yellow figures" of socialism extinguish one another. None of these forms of economic and political organization seem

4

tolerable: the billionaire-worker in *Gas II* is the "new man" who accepts the inevitable "eccentricity" of an absolute conviction of human integrity. He knows that he must continue to proclaim it as a platonic truth, an "inner realm" of meaning, to which any future must refer.

Thus the central motif of these three plays is the clash between a stubbornly maintained vision of truth and the seductive and often overwhelming compulsions of power—the power of individual satisfaction, the power of wealth, and power in its harshest and most technical modern form, exercised for its own sake.

It is true that Kaiser insists that "the deepest wisdom is found only by a single mind. And when it is found it is so overwhelming that it cannot become effective." Yet, the issue which Kaiser argues concerns all of us, it is not a private one; its moral impact cannot therefore, as in the plays of Ibsen and Hauptmann, be shown in a series of individual experiences with which we as spectators might identify ourselves. Indeed, Kaiser is not primarily concerned with the alternatives of action or judgment that might be open to a well-defined character; his purpose is altogether the unraveling of the implications of an intellectual position. Each turn of events, every sentence that is uttered, is, therefore, in Kaiser's plays, a key to an essentially dialectical intention. His plots are exactly developed elaborations of his central ideas. This is to say that the dramatic structure of the *Gas* trilogy is determined not so much by the logic of individual, or group, psychology, as by the logic—we might almost say, logistics—of an idea. All of Kaiser's works are masterpieces of deduction: "To write a play," Kaiser himself suggested, "is to pursue an idea to the end."

This deliberate narrowing of the dramatic intent has its striking consequences for the form of Kaiser's plays. Where intellectual and emotional tensions are to be stated with the utmost concentration a high degree of abstraction becomes inevitable. Instead of the ample and detailed setting of the naturalistic theater, Kaiser employs few but emphatic properties in an otherwise bleak and pointedly inhuman stage space. His figures are far from the psychologically plausible characters of the realistic drama; they are, rather, nameless and puppet-like cyphers, symbols of family or class relationships who are at times distinguished only by arbitrary colors and who seem to carry the argument all the more efficiently the less specific their individuality.

The same sort of reduction to a minimum of naturalness is characteristic of Kaiser's language: what is said by each of these schematic figures is tense and abrupt, and in syntax and vocabulary stripped of all leisurely irrelevancy. Whether we listen to the technical jargon of the engineer or to the anxious and more and more resolute voice of the "billionaire," we are always aware of that remarkable sense of direction with which Kaiser pursues his argument. The form of the dialogue is equally revealing: instead of justifying the actions of individual characters it seems rather to plot out the relay stations of the dramatic idea. This is perhaps nowhere more evident than in those passages where, for an extreme measure of antithetical speech, Kaiser resorts to the classical device of stichomythy.

Deliberate sparseness and economy of setting, figure, and language corresponds to the precision with which the play as a whole is designed. We need only analyze with some care the fourth act of *Gas I* to recognize Kaiser's craftsmanship, his use of the fugal structure, and his skill in organizing, through sound and light and a careful manipulation of group movements, a slowly rising crescendo of urgency.

Kaiser's incomparable instinct for the theatrical effect is one of his greatest assets. Indeed, it saves his plays on the one hand from becoming mere intellectual exercises in the hands of an accomplished "Denkspieler"; and on the other from that excess of exclamatory feeling which is typical of much expressionist writing. Kaiser's passion is directed toward the illumination of rational and, therefore, arguable human alternatives; his utopian vision of the "new man" is not vague and sentimental but amouts to a calculated appraisal of the energies of heart and mind and action which the human being must marshal for his own salvation. We cannot read the final speech of the "billion-

6

aire," or the second act of *Gas II*, without being moved by the superb pathos of the moralist. Here, as in the plays of Lessing or Schiller, with whom Kaiser has in form and in substance so much in common, the work of art offers us a most articulate and compelling assertion of the humanistic faith.

VICTOR LANGE

SUGGESTED READING

Columbia Dictionary of Modern European Literature. pp. 343-345. New York, 1947.

Diebald, B. *Der Denkspieler Georg Kaiser.* Frankfurt, 1924.

Elbe, A. M. Technische und soziale Probleme in der Dramen-struktur Georg Kaisers. Diss. Cologne, 1959.

Fivian, E. A. *Georg Kaiser* (in German). Munich, 1946.

Frenz, H. "Georg Kaiser" in *Poet Lore.* 1946. 363-369.

Freyhan, M. *Georg Kaisers Werk.* Berlin, 1926.

Fruchter, M. J. *The Social Dialectic in Georg Kaiser's Dramatic Works.* Philadelphia, 1933.

Kenworthy, B. J. *Georg Kaiser,* 1957.

Paulsen, W. *Georg Kaiser,* 1960.

Twentieth-Century Authors, pp. 742f. New York, 1942.

PERSONS

The Gentleman in White.
The Billionaire's Son.
The Daughter.
The Officer.
The Engineer.
First Gentleman in Black.
Second Gentleman in Black.
Third Gentleman in Black.
Fourth Gentleman in Black.
Fifth Gentleman in Black.
Government Commissioner.
The Clerk.
First Workman.
Second Workman.
Third Workman.
The Girl.
The Woman.
The Mother.
The Captain.
A Machine-gun Detachment, Workmen,
    Workwomen.

G A S

FIRST ACT

A vast square room, all in white, the office of the Billionaire's Son. The rear wall is composed entirely of glass in large squares. The walls to right and left are covered from floor to ceiling with great charts bearing statistics, scales and diagrams in black and white. To the left is a spacious desk and an arm-chair of austere design, a second arm-chair at the side. A smaller desk to the right. Visible through the glass wall in a murky violet light, the steep close-thronged shapes of great chimney-stacks from which flame and smoke pour in horizontal lines.

Faint bursts of music come and go.

A young Clerk at the smaller desk to the right.

Enter noiselessly the Gentleman in White, a strange, whimsical, phantom figure, entirely in white, including a chalk-white face. He shuts the door noiselessly, surveys the room, tip-toes towards the Clerk, touches him upon the shoulder.

9

GENTLEMAN IN WHITE: Music?

THE CLERK *turns up a startled face to him.*

GENTLEMAN IN WHITE *listens to sounds from overhead, and nods:* Valse.

CLERK: How do you happen——?

GENTLEMAN IN WHITE: Quite casually. A certain noiselessness—achieved by rubber soles. (*He seats himself in chair before desk and crosses his legs.*) The Chief?—busy? Upstairs?

CLERK: What do you wish?

GENTLEMAN IN WHITE: A dancing party?

CLERK (*in growing haste and confusion*): There's a wedding—overhead.

GENTLEMAN IN WHITE (*with pointing finger*): The Chief—or—?

CLERK: The Daughter—and the Officer.

GENTLEMAN IN WHITE: Then, of course, he can't be seen at present—the Chief?

CLERK: We have no chief—*here——*

GENTLEMAN IN WHITE (*switching round*): Interesting! Assuming that you are not too deeply engaged in delicate calculations—the wage-schedules there——?

CLERK: We have no wage-schedules—*here!*

GENTLEMAN IN WHITE: That piles up the interest. That touches the core of things. (*Pointing through the window.*) This gigantic establishment going full blast—and no chief —no wage-schedules—— ?

CLERK: We work—and we share!

GENTLEMAN IN WHITE (*pointing to the wall*): The diagrams ? (*Rising and reading the tables.*) Three divisions. Up to thirty years, Scale One. Up to forty years, Scale Two. Over forty, Scale Three. A simple bit of arithmetic. Profit-sharing according to age. (*To Clerk.*) An invention of your Chief?—who refuses to be a chief ?

CLERK: Because he does not wish to be richer than others!

GENTLEMAN IN WHITE: Was he ever rich ?

CLERK: He is the son of the Billionaire!

GENTLEMAN IN WHITE (*smiling*): So he advanced to the very periphery of wealth and then returned to its centre—to its core——. And you work ?

CLERK: Every man works to his utmost!

GENTLEMAN IN WHITE: Because you get your share of the total earnings ?

CLERK: Yes—and that's why we work harder here than anywhere else on earth!

GENTLEMAN IN WHITE: I suppose you produce something worth such an effort ?

CLERK: Gas!

THE GENTLEMAN IN WHITE *blows through his hollowed hand.*

CLERK (*excited*): Haven't you heard of the Gas we produce?

THE GENTLEMAN IN WHITE *also shows excitement.*

CLERK: Coal-and-water-power are out of date. This new source of energy drives millions of machines at super-speed. We furnish the power. Our Gas feeds the industry of the entire world!

GENTLEMAN IN WHITE (*at window*): Day and night—fire and smoke?

CLERK: We have attained the acme of our achievement!

GENTLEMAN IN WHITE (*returning*): Because poverty is abolished?

CLERK: Our intensive efforts create—create!

GENTLEMAN IN WHITE: Because profits are shared?

CLERK: Gas!

GENTLEMAN IN WHITE: And suppose sometime the Gas—should——

CLERK: The work must go on—not a moment's pause! We are working for ourselves—not for the pockets of others. No loafing—no strikes. The work goes on without a pause. There will always be Gas!

GENTLEMAN IN WHITE: And suppose sometime the Gas should—explode?

THE CLERK *stares at him.*

GENTLEMAN IN WHITE: What then?

THE CLERK *is speechless.*

THE GENTLEMAN IN WHITE *breathes the words directly into his face.* The White Horror! (*Rising to full height and listening to sounds overhead.*) Music. (*Halting half-way to door.*) Valse. (*Trips out, silently.*)

CLERK (*in growing consternation, finally seizes telephone, almost screaming*): The Engineer! (*His eyes dart back and forth between the doors to right and left.*)

(*The Engineer enters from right, wearing a frock-coat.*)

ENGINEER: What——

(*A Workman in white blouse comes in from the left, greatly excited.*)

CLERK (*pointing with outstretched arm at Workman*): There——!

ENGINEER (*to Workman*): Are you looking for me?

WORKMAN (*surprised*): I was just coming to report to you.

ENGINEER (*to Clerk*): But you had already telephoned me!

CLERK: Because——

ENGINEER: Did you receive a report?

CLERK (*shakes his head and points to Workman*): This man——

ENGINEER: Has just come.

CLERK:——was bound to come!

ENGINEER (*somehow disquieted*): What has happened?

WORKMAN: The Gas in the sight-tube shows colour.

ENGINEER: Colour!

WORKMAN: It is still only a tinge.

ENGINEER: Growing deeper?

WORKMAN: Visibly.

ENGINEER: What colour?

WORKMAN: A light rose.

ENGINEER: Are you not mistaken?

WORKMAN: I have been watching it carefully.

ENGINEER: How long?

CLERK (*impulsively*): Ten minutes?

WORKMAN: Yes.

ENGINEER: How do *you* know that?

CLERK: Wouldn't it be best to ring up—upstairs?

ENGINEER (*telephones*): Engineer. Report from Central Station—sight-tube shows colour.

14

I'll inspect personally. (*To Workman*): Come along. (*Both go out.*)

CLERK (*suddenly throws up his arms, then runs out screaming*): We're done for—we're done for! (*From the right the Billionaire's Son—sixty years old—and the Officer in red uniform come in.*)

OFFICER: Is there any cause for serious alarm?

BILLIONAIRE'S SON: I am waiting for the Engineer's report. Nevertheless, I am glad you are both going. I wanted to say a word about the fortune which my daughter is bringing you. (*Takes a note-book out of his writing-table.*)

OFFICER: I thank you.

BILLIONAIRE'S SON: You need not thank me. It is her mother's money. It ought to be considerable. I have no mind for such things.

OFFICER: An officer is forced——

BILLIONAIRE'S SON: You love each other—I offered no objection.

OFFICER: I shall guard your daughter, whom you are confiding to my hands, as I would my own honour.

BILLIONAIRE'S SON (*opening book*): Here is the amount of the funds and where they are deposited. Select an efficient banker and take his advice. That is most necessary.

OFFICER (*reads, then in amazement*): We shall certainly require a banker to manage all this!

BILLIONAIRE'S SON: Because the capital is a large one? I did not mean it that way.

OFFICER: I do not understand.

BILLIONAIRE'S SON: What you have now you have for the entire future. You must not expect anything from me. Not now and not later. I shall leave nothing. My principles are sufficiently well known—they must also be familiar to you.

OFFICER: It is not likely that we——

BILLIONAIRE'S SON: No one can tell. As long as money is piled up, money will go, lost. Conditions based on money are always uncertain. I feel I must tell you this, so that later on I may feel no responsibility. You have married the daughter of a workman—I am nothing more. I will not conceal from you the fact that I would rather that my daughter's mother had not left her a fortune. But I exercise authority only in my own province, and I never attempt to force anyone into this. Not even my daughter.

(*The Daughter, in travelling dress, comes in from the right.*)

DAUGHTER: Why must we hurry off this way?

OFFICER (*kissing her hand*): How warm you still are from the dance!

BILLIONAIRE'S SON: I should not like the marriage-festival to end in a discord. (*They start.*) The danger can be, no doubt, averted. But it demands every possible effort.

DAUGHTER (*at window*): Below—in the works?

BILLIONAIRE'S SON: I should not find time to say good-bye—later on.

DAUGHTER: Is it so very serious?

OFFICER: Counter measures have been taken.

BILLIONAIRE'S SON (*taking Daughter's hand*): *Bon voyage.* Be happy. To-day you have laid aside my name. That is no loss. I am a man of plain tastes. I cannot approach the splendour of your new name. Must you and all you are be extinguished in me—now that you are going?

THE DAUGHTER *looks at him questioningly.*

OFFICER: How can you say that?

BILLIONAIRE'S SON: I cannot follow you in your world—a world of fallacies.

DAUGHTER: But I shall return.

BILLIONAIRE'S SON: It is not likely that I can wait for a real return. (*Abruptly.*) I shall now ask the guests to leave. (*He kisses her forehead. The Daughter stands deeply moved. He clasps the Officer's hand. The Officer leads the Daughter out.*)

BILLIONAIRE'S SON (*telephones*): Tell the people in the drawing-room that a disturbance at the works necessitates bringing the festivities to a close. It is advisable to leave the vicinity as quickly as possible. (*The music ceases.*)

(*Enter Engineer from left. A working-coat over his dress suit. He is deeply agitated.*)

ENGINEER (*gasping*): Report from Central Station—Gas colours deeper every second. In a few minutes—at the same rate of progress—it will be—a deep red!

BILLIONAIRE'S SON: Is anything wrong with the engines?

ENGINEER: All working perfectly!

BILLIONAIRE'S SON: Any trouble with the ingredients?

ENGINEER: All ingredients, all!—tested before mixing!

BILLIONAIRE'S SON: Where does the fault lie?

ENGINEER (*shaking from top to toe*): In—the formula!

BILLIONAIRE'S SON: Your formula—does not—work out?

ENGINEER: My formula—does not—work out!

BILLIONAIRE'S SON: Are you sure?

ENGINEER: Yes! *Now!*

BILLIONAIRE'S SON: Have you found the mistake?

ENGINEER: No!

BILLIONAIRE'S SON: Can't you find it?

ENGINEER: The calculation is—correct!

BILLIONAIRE'S SON: And yet the sight-tubes show colour?

THE ENGINEER *throws himself into chair before desk and jerks his hand across sheet of paper.*

BILLIONAIRE'S SON: Have the alarms been set going?

ENGINEER (*without pausing in his work*): All the bells are pounding away.

BILLIONAIRE'S SON: Is there enough time to clear the works?

ENGINEER: The lorries are whizzing from door to door.

BILLIONAIRE'S SON: In good order?

ENGINEER: In perfect order!

BILLIONAIRE'S SON (*in terrible agitation*): Will all get out?

ENGINEER (*leaping to his feet, standing erect before him*): I have done my duty—the formula is clear—without a flaw!

BILLIONAIRE'S SON (*stunned*): You cannot find the error?

ENGINEER: Nobody can find it. Nobody! No brain could reckon more carefully. I've made the final calculation!

BILLIONAIRE'S SON: And it does not work out?

Engineer: It works out—and does not work
out. We have reached the limit—works out and
does not work out. Figures fail us—works out—
yet does not work out. The thing sums itself up,
and then turns against us—works out and does
not work out!

Billionaire's Son: The Gas——?

Engineer: It is bleeding in the sight-tube!
Flooding past the formula—going red in the
sight-glass. Floating out of the formula—taking
the bit in its own teeth. I have done my duty.
My head is quite clear. The impossible is going
to take place—it cannot come—yet it is coming!

Billionaire's Son (*feeling for a chair*): We are
helpless—delivered up to——

Engineer: The Explosion!

(*A terrible sibilance tears asunder the silence
without. A grinding thunder bursts—the smoke-
stacks crack and fall. A silence, empty and smokeless,
ensues. The great glass windows rattle into the
room in a cascade of fragments.*)

Billionaire's Son (*flattened against the wall—
in a toneless voice*): The earth swayed——

Engineer: Pressure of millions of atmos-
pheres——

Billionaire's Son: All is silent—a grave.

Engineer: Immense radius of devastation——

BILLIONAIRE'S SON: Who is still living?

(*The door to left is flung open: a Workman—naked —stained by the explosion—totters in.*)

WORKMAN: Report from Shed Eight—Central —white cat burst—red eyes torn open—yellow mouth gaping—humps up crackling back—grows round—snaps away girders—lifts up roof— bursts—sparks! sparks! (*Sitting down in the middle of floor and striking about him*): Chase away the cat—Shoo! Shoo!—smash her jaws—Shoo! Shoo!—bury her eyes—they flame—hammer down her back—hammer it down—thousands of fists! It's swelling, swelling—growing fat— fatter—Gas out of every crack—every tube! (*Once more half erecting himself*): Report from Central—the white cat has—exploded! (*He collapses and lies prone.*)

BILLIONAIRE'S SON *goes to him.*

THE WORKMAN *gropes with his hand.*

BILLIONAIRE'S SON *takes his hand.*

WORKMAN (*with a cry*): Mother! (*Dies.*)

BILLIONAIRE'S SON (*bending low above him*): O man! O mankind!

SECOND ACT

The same room. A green jalousie or blind has been let down over the great window. In front of this stands a long draughting-table covered with drawings.

The young Clerk—with hair which has now grown snow-white—at his table, inactive.

The Billionaire's Son is leaning against the draughting-table.

BILLIONAIRE'S SON: How long since it happened?

CLERK: Just seventeen days ago to-day.

BILLIONAIRE'S SON (*turning and looking at the window*): Formerly great sheds stood there and thrust smoke-stacks against the heavens—belching a fiery breath. That was what we used to see behind this green shutter—not so?

CLERK: Everything pulverized to dust—in a few minutes.

BILLIONAIRE'S SON: Are you sure it did not take place a thousand years ago?

22

CLERK: I shall never forget that day!

BILLIONAIRE'S SON: Perhaps this day is already too far distant for you?

THE CLERK *looks at him questioningly.*

BILLIONAIRE'S SON: That is to say—when you look at your hair?

CLERK: I was beside myself—it was almost hallucination. I felt it in my bones that it was coming. I saw Horror—saw it bodily. And that was worse—than what really happened! And I grew white before it really happened.

BILLIONAIRE'S SON (*nodding*): The White Horror—this was necessary in order to give us impetus—a powerful impetus—to fling us forward for a thousand years! Seventeen days, you say? Seventeen days full of peace and quiet.

CLERK (*in a matter-of-fact manner*): The workmen still persist in their refusal.

BILLIONAIRE'S SON: And I cannot employ them. The works have been levelled to the ground.

CLERK: They will not take up work before——

BILLIONAIRE'S SON: Before I give my permission.

CLERK (*nonplussed*): Are you postponing the rebuilding?

BILLIONAIRE'S SON (*shaking his head*): I am not postponing it——

23

CLERK: You are always at work upon the drawings.

BILLIONAIRE'S SON (*bending over the draughting-table*): I am measuring—and colouring——

CLERK: The whole world is in urgent need of Gas—the demand is imperative. The supplies will soon be exhausted. If the Gas should— come to an end——!

BILLIONAIRE'S SON (*quickly erecting himself*): Then I hold the fate of the world in my hands.

CLERK: You must grant the demands of the workmen—or else the most terrible catastrophe of all will come!

BILLIONAIRE'S SON (*walks towards him and strokes his hair*): A catastrophe you call it?—you youthful whitehead? *You* should have had your warning. It was terrible enough when everything went up in thunder about us here. Do you wish to return to the White Horror? Are your fingers itching to play at the same old game? Can't you be anything but a Clerk?

CLERK: I have my calling.

BILLIONAIRE'S SON: Don't you feel the call— for something more important?

CLERK: I must earn my living.

BILLIONAIRE'S SON: And what if this particular " must " should be done away with?

24

CLERK: I am a Clerk.

BILLIONAIRE'S SON: From the crown of your head to the sole of your feet?

CLERK: I —am a Clerk.

BILLIONAIRE'S SON: Because you have always been a Clerk?

CLERK: It is—my calling.

BILLIONAIRE'S SON (*smiling*): Ah, it has buried you deep indeed. The strata of society are carried upon you—layer by layer. Nothing less than an exploding volcano will bring you to the surface—nothing less than this can teach you to rise.

Three Workmen enter from the left.

BILLIONAIRE'S SON (*addressing them*): Have you once more come stamping through the dêbris? I have not yet been able to send you my reply. The thing is still taking shape— I am up to the ears in sketches and calculations —look here! But I can make you a definite proposal if you will grant me a final time limit. Are you willing?

FIRST WORKMAN: The excitement——

BILLIONAIRE'S SON: I understand. There were many victims—I do not dare to think of how many victims the accident . claimed. (*Clasping his head with his hands.*) And yet I must keep them clearly before me. My decision will then be clear. Speak.

FIRST WORKMAN: We are merely making the same demand which we have always made.

BILLIONAIRE'S SON: I know what it is. I am revolving it in my mind. I am taking it as the basis of my—— (*Abruptly.*) I am supposed to send away the Engineer?

FIRST WORKMAN: There is still time—to-day.

BILLIONAIRE'S SON: And to-morrow?

FIRST WORKMAN: To-morrow we would refuse to take up work for a period of twenty weeks.

BILLIONAIRE'S SON: Leaving the wreckage lie?

FIRST WORKMAN: In case of a settlement the works could be set going again—in twenty weeks.

SECOND WORKMAN: The world's supply of Gas will not last longer than twenty weeks.

THIRD WORKMAN: There will be a world-wide holiday.

BILLIONAIRE'S SON: . . . Why should I let the Engineer go? (*The Workmen are silent.*) Where lies his fault? Did the safety appliances fail to work? Even in a slight degree? Were the alarm signals incomplete? In making concessions to you, 1 must also be just to him. That is no more than right.

THIRD WORKMAN: The Gas exploded.

BILLIONAIRE'S SON: Was it his fault? No. The formula was correct. It is still correct.

FIRST WORKMAN: The Explosion came.

BILLIONAIRE'S SON: According to its own laws. Not his.

SECOND WORKMAN: He made the formula.

BILLIONAIRE'S SON: No man could make a safer one!

(The three Workmen are silent.)

FIRST WORKMAN: The Engineer must go!

SECOND WORKMAN: He must go to-day!

THIRD WORKMAN: His going must be announced at once!

FIRST WORKMAN: We must take this announcement back with us.

BILLIONAIRE'S SON: *Must* you have your sacrifice? Is that everything? Do you think that you can thereby silence the dead who call aloud in you? Do you think that you can strangle that which clamours in your blood? Can you hide a field of corpses under new corpses? Are you entangled in this horrible lust of revenge after all the horrors which have been? Is this

27

the fruit of the fiery tree which rained pitch and brimstone upon us?

First Workman: There is also this—we can no longer be responsible for the attitude of the workers.

Second Workman: There is a fermentation—which is growing.

Third Workman: There will be an outbreak.

Billionaire's Son (*violently*): Tell them—all, all of them—that they have ears to hear and a brain to reason with. The thing passed beyond the limits of the human. The brain of the Engineer had calculated everything to the utmost. But beyond this there rule forces which suffer no rule. The flaw lies in eternity. Impossible to find by mortal means. The formula tallies—yet the Gas explodes. Can you not understand?

First Workman: We have our orders.

Billionaire's Son: Will you also assume the responsibility?

First Workman: For what?

Billionaire's Son: If I grant your demand—if I let the Engineer go—and you return to work——

First Workman: We'll pledge ourselves to that.

Billionaire's Son: And you will make Gas?

Second and Third Workman: Gas!

Billionaire's Son: The formula will be used?

First Workman (*hesitating*): If it is correct——

Billionaire's Son: Incontrovertibly so!

Second Workman: It is correct and——

Billionaire's Son: And the Gas exploded.

(*The three Workmen are silent.*)

Billionaire's Son: And, therefore, must not the Engineer remain?

(*The three Workmen stare in front of them.*)

Billionaire's Son: Is not my refusal a safe-guard against horror? Am I not keeping a door shut, a door behind which hell is smouldering? A door which leaves no way open to life? It is like a burning cul-de-sac. Who would go into a cul-de-sac? and lose sight of his goal? Who would be such a fool as to batter his forehead against the last wall and say: I have reached the end. He has reached the end, it is true, but this end is Annihilation. Turn back! turn back! you have heard the warning thundered from the heavens—it rent the air and came crashing down upon us. Turn back! turn back!

First Workman (*erecting himself*): We must work!

Second Workman: And our work is here!

THIRD WORKMAN: We are workers!

BILLIONAIRE'S SON: You are workers—indefatigably so. Caught up in the maelstrom of the ultimate effort. Immeasurably enthusiastic over all this. (*Pointing to the charts and tables.*) There we have the mad chase—all the diagrams. Your work—and your wages in the hollow of your hands. That cheers you up—that spurs you on beyond even profit—that makes you work for work's sake. It is like an outbreak of fever, and it clouds the senses. Work—work—a wedge that is driven forward and which bores because it bores. To what end? I bore because I bore— I was a borer—I am a borer—and I remain a borer! Doesn't this make you shiver? Shiver at thought of the mutilation you inflict upon yourselves? You living, sentient, wonderful beings—you manifold ones—you men!

FIRST WORKMAN: We must take back a clear reply.

BILLIONAIRE'S SON: I have given you one. But you do not yet understand. And it is also new to me—to me who feel my way so slowly and carefully.

SECOND WORKMAN: Is the Engineer going?

BILLIONAIRE'S SON: He is going.

THIRD WORKMAN: To-day?

BILLIONAIRE'S SON: He is not going!

FIRST WORKMAN: We do not understand.

BILLIONAIRE'S SON: He goes—and he remains
—the Engineer must become a matter of utter
indifference to us.

SECOND WORKMAN: What does this mean?

BILLIONAIRE'S SON: That is still a small and
precious secret of mine. I shall reveal it to you—
later on. Look at those plans—I did not finish
them—because the help I need is not yet at hand
—and this help I can obtain only from the man
who is and is not your enemy.

FIRST WORKMAN: May we give a definite
answer to our fellows out there?

BILLIONAIRE'S SON: Whatever you please. I
will carry out everything—and more than you
can promise your fellows out there. So now you
may depart—in contentment.

(*The three Workmen go out.*)

BILLIONAIRE'S SON *bends over the drawings on
the draughting-table.*

CLERK (*leaping up from his chair, hurriedly*):
I—am going!

BILLIONAIRE'S SON *rising to an erect position.*

CLERK: I am—out of work.

BILLIONAIRE'S SON: For the present.

CLERK: But there will be no change!

31

BILLIONAIRE'S SON: Visions again? But of a somewhat darker shade this time? No mirage with a green oasis rising from the desert? Prophecy, my young prophetic friend. You have a most peculiar gift. I am curious to hear your prophecies.

CLERK: I—there is nothing more to write about.

BILLIONAIRE'S SON: Can nothing tempt you? Are you not eager for health? Would you not like to work with both hands, instead of this right hand of yours which does nothing but write? you with the lamed left?

CLERK: I—am going!

BILLIONAIRE'S SON: Whither?

CLERK: To the others!

BILLIONAIRE'S SON: Gather together and growl before the gates. The wheels are still spinning in your breasts—the urge is still too great. It will require time before inertia can set in. And then I'll admit you all.

CLERK *goes out to the right.*

BILLIONAIRE'S SON *once more at the draughting-table. Enter Engineer from the left.*

BILLIONAIRE'S SON (*looks up and regards him quizzically*): No damage? in body or clothes?

ENGINEER *looks at him questioningly.*

32

BILLIONAIRE'S SON: Are you not the scapegoat who is to be impaled on his own horns? Haven't they beaten you yet?

ENGINEER: I heard them hissing.

BILLIONAIRE'S SON: That was only the signal for the bleeding sacrifice—the slaughter takes place to-morrow.

ENGINEER: I know that I am free of careless-ness—or incapacity.

BILLIONAIRE'S SON: But they are after your scalp.

ENGINEER: These people ought to be shown——

BILLIONAIRE'S SON: . . . That a proof is clear and yet is not clear.

ENGINEER: I cannot leave—it would be like a confession of guilt——

BILLIONAIRE'S SON: Could I not discharge you?

ENGINEER: No! For you would then brand me with the mark—which makes me an outcast.

BILLIONAIRE'S SON: One must suffer for many.

ENGINEER (*excitedly*): Yes—if one would serve the advantage of the many. But where is the advantage here? Take this man or that man and put him in my place—the formula remains valid —must remain so. He must reckon with human reason, and human reason reckons only in this way. Or you must make Gas by means of a weaker formula.

BILLIONAIRE'S SON: Do you believe in a weaker formula?

ENGINEER: All the machinery of the world would have to be rebuilt.

BILLIONAIRE'S SON: That would not prevent its coming to pass.

ENGINEER: Facing the necessity of an inferior motive power——

BILLIONAIRE'S SON: The machines might be stopped—but not men.

ENGINEER: But after they have learned the danger?

BILLIONAIRE'S SON: And no matter if they were blown up ten times, they would establish themselves in the burning zone for the eleventh time.

ENGINEER: An explosion such as this——

BILLIONAIRE'S SON: Will bring them to their senses, you think? Has it had any influence upon the fever which makes them rave? They are already clamouring out there: hand the Engineer over to us—and then we'll speed on again——out of one explosion into another explosion.

ENGINEER: And, therefore, my leaving is senseless.

34

BILLIONAIRE'S SON (*smiling craftily*): It would be an unparalleled stupidity! They would merely come jumping into the witches' cauldron once more—the rogues. The gates must be blocked, and I intend to use you for that purpose. I am powerful, now that I am going to keep you by me.

ENGINEER (*stroking his forehead*): But, what are you going——

BILLIONAIRE'S SON: Come here. (*He takes him to the draughting-table.*) Do you see this? Sketches—rough sketches. The first draft of a new project. Merely hints of something big, something momentous—the first sketches.

ENGINEER: What is that?

BILLIONAIRE'S SON: Don't you recognise the land?

ENGINEER: The plant?

BILLIONAIRE'S SON: Has been levelled to the ground.

ENGINEER: Are these the new sheds?

BILLIONAIRE'S SON: What! of such ridiculous dimensions!

ENGINEER: Are these yards?

BILLIONAIRE'S SON: The coloured circles?

ENGINEER: Are these railway tracks?

BILLIONAIRE'S SON: These green lines? (*The Engineer stares at the plans.*) Can't you guess? Have you no suspicions? You sly duck! You feeder on figures! Are you puzzled by this many-coloured riddle? You are blind—colour-blind from the eternal monotony of your doings—up to this very day. Now a new day is born to greet you, and smiles upon you like springtime. Open your eyes and let them sweep over this domain. The vari-coloured earth is all about you (*pointing to the plans.*) The green lines—streets bordered by trees. The red, the yellow, the blue circles—open spaces full of flowering plants, sprouting from smooth lawns. The squares—houses, human dwellings with a small holding of land—shelters. Mighty streets go forth here—penetrating, conquering other domains, great roads trodden by pilgrims, our pilgrims, who shall preach simplicity—to us—to all!

(*His gestures are grandiose.*)

ENGINEER (*puzzled*): Do you intend to re-build the plant—somewhere?——

BILLIONAIRE'S SON: It buried itself. It reached its apex and then collapsed. And that is why we are discharged—you and I and all the others—discharged with clear consciences. We went our way to the very end without fear—and now we turn aside. It is no more than our right—our honest right.

ENGINEER: The reconstruction—is doubtful?

BILLIONAIRE'S SON (*patting the plans with his his hand*): The decision is here and it is *against* reconstruction.

ENGINEER: And the Gas—which can be made only here?

BILLIONAIRE'S SON: The Gas exploded.

ENGINEER: The workmen?

BILLIONAIRE'S SON: Homesteaders—each on his patch of green.

ENGINEER: That—is—impossible!

BILLIONAIRE'S SON: Do you object to my plans? I told you that they were incomplete. I have counted upon you to help me carry them out. I am counting greatly upon your help. There is no other man so capable of carrying out a big project as yourself. I have the deepest confidence in you. Shall we proceed to work?

(*He draws up a stool to the draughting-table and sits down.*)

ENGINEER (*making a few steps backward*): But I am an Engineer!

BILLIONAIRE'S SON: You will find excellent use for your capacities here.

ENGINEER: That is not—my branch.

37

BILLIONAIRE'S SON: All branches are united in this.

ENGINEER: I cannot undertake such a task.

BILLIONAIRE'S SON: Is it too difficult for you?

ENGINEER: Too—pitiful!

BILLIONAIRE'S SON (*rising*): That do you say? You think this trivial—you with your genius for figures! Are you the slave of your calculations? Are you fettered to those girders which you constructed? Have you delivered up your arms and legs, your blood and your senses to this frame which you devised? Are you a diagram covered with a skin? (*He reaches out for him.*) Where are *you*? Your human warmth? your beating pulse? your sense of shame?

ENGINEER: If I cannot be occupied—in my own line——

BILLIONAIRE'S SON: Your hands should muzzle your mouth—for it is talking murder.

ENGINEER: . . . Then I must ask for my dismissal.

BILLIONAIRE'S SON (*supporting himself against the table*): No! *that* will bring back the others. The road would be clear and they would come storming back, and build up their hell again—and the fever will continue to rage. Help me!
38

stay by me! Work here with me—here where
I am working.

ENGINEER: I am dismissed!

BILLIONAIRE'S SON *regards him speechlessly.*

ENGINEER *goes out to the right.*

BILLIONAIRE'S SON (*strong at last*): Then I must
force, must force you—every one of you!

THIRD ACT

An oval room. There is a high wainscot of white-enamelled wood. In this there are two invisible doors, two at the rear—one to the left. In the centre there is a small round table covered with a green cloth. This is surrounded by six chairs, close together.

The Officer enters from the left—in a military cape. He can scarcely control his emotion. He looks for the doors, taps parts of the wainscot.

The Billionaire's Son enters from the left, to the rear.

OFFICER (*turning swiftly about and advancing*): Am I disturbing you?

BILLIONAIRE'S SON (*astonished*): Have you two come back?

OFFICER: No, I've come back alone.

BILLIONAIRE'S SON: Where is your wife?

OFFICER: She—was not able to accompany me.

BILLIONAIRE'S SON: Is she ill—my daughter?

OFFICER: She—does not know I've come here!

BILLIONAIRE'S SON (*nodding*): The looks of

things here are certainly far from edifying. The paternal foundation is now only a mass of ruins. Would you like to have a look round?

OFFICER (*hastily*): The catastrophe must have been terrible. I suppose the rebuilding is going ahead at a good pace?

BILLIONAIRE'S SON: Have you noticed anything of the the sort going on?

OFFICER: It is natural—and you must be immensely busy.

BILLIONAIRE'S SON (*shaking his head*): My time——

OFFICER: You are more than busy. The work is more than you can manage. (*Pointing to the table.*) There is going to be a meeting. I am sorry to be forced to disturb you. (*Suddenly, almost abruptly*). But I must ask you to give me a little of your time—now!

BILLIONAIRE'S SON: All things are equally important to me.

OFFICER: I thank you for your willingness to hear me. The matter concerns me—concerns my salvation, my rescue——

BILLIONAIRE'S SON: Salvation? rescue? from what?

OFFICER: From being cashiered from the regiment—in disgrace.

BILLIONAIRE'S SON: Why?

OFFICER: I've contracted debts—at cards—debts of honour. And I must pay them by to-morrow noon.

BILLIONAIRE'S SON: Can't you pay them?

OFFICER: No!

BILLIONAIRE'S SON: If it is necessary—draw upon your fortune—your wife's dowry.

OFFICER: That—no longer exists.

BILLIONAIRE'S SON: What has become of it?

OFFICER (*excitedly*): I played and I lost. I tried to cover the losses and began to speculate. The speculations were a failure and involved great losses. I increased my stakes at the table beyond my means—and if I cannot pay—I—must—blow—out—my brains!

BILLIONAIRE'S SON (*after a pause*): And so your final way leads you to me?

OFFICER: It cost me a great effort to come here—to you—who have confided in me, and whom I have deceived. But despair drives me to you. I deserve your reproaches—all the blame you can pour upon me is just blame. I have nothing to say in my defence.

BILLIONAIRE'S SON: I do not reproach you.

OFFICER (*reaching for his hand*): I am

shamed by your goodness—your forgiveness. I swear that—once I get out of this safely—I——

BILLIONAIRE'S SON: I do not wish you to swear——

OFFICER: Then I will pledge myself——

BILLIONAIRE'S SON: Because I cannot do you a service——

OFFICER (*stares at him*): Will you not——

BILLIONAIRE'S SON: I cannot help—even though I would. I told you at the time that you were marrying the daughter of a workman. I am that workman. I hid nothing from you. I gave you a clear idea of everything.

OFFICER: Means are everywhere at your disposal!

BILLIONAIRE'S SON: No.

OFFICER: A word from you—and every bank is at your service.

BILLIONAIRE'S SON: No longer to-day.

OFFICER: The great plant—surely that will be working again in a few weeks——

BILLIONAIRE'S SON: It will be standing still!

OFFICER: Still——?

BILLIONAIRE'S SON: Yes, I have come to other conclusions. Will you help me? I need help—much help. The great stronghold of error cannot be toppled over by one man alone—a thousand hands must help to shake it.

OFFICER (*bewildered*): You will not help——?

BILLIONAIRE'S SON: I am myself in need. A good wind brings you hither. You are a debtor —as I am a debtor. And we are both guiltless. But now lips are loosened and accusations pour forth—accusations against all of us.

OFFICER (*clutching his head with his hands*): I— can—not—think——

BILLIONAIRE'S SON: Take off that gaudy uniform and put aside your sword. You are a good man—for did not my daughter become your wife? You are sound at heart. Whence came this shadow? Whence all that hides and covers up your real self? How did you succumb to this temptation for show?

OFFICER: What!—you expect me to give up my career as an officer——?

BILLIONAIRE'S SON: Confess your fault—and prove your guiltlessness. See that you win the eyes and ears of men—see that your voice carries farther and farther. I myself cannot realise myself—I remain disguised for life in this coat. And so the currents of the great forces in me are turned awry—turned into a canal full of deeds undone—because one deed still threatens—a deed

44

which will bring annihilation in its train. I would save those who would bring about something which can only bring about ruin.

OFFICER (*suppressing a groan*): Can—you help me ?

BILLIONAIRE'S SON: Yes!

OFFICER: Then give me——!

BILLIONAIRE'S SON: That which *you* give me I could never pay for.

OFFICER: My period of grace is expiring.

BILLIONAIRE'S SON: No, it will go on for ever.

OFFICER: Money!

BILLIONAIRE'S SON: Ought I to cheat you with money—cheat you out of your real self ?

OFFICER (*in desperation*): I must leave the Service—I shall be struck off the Rolls—I——

BILLIONAIRE'S SON (*leading him towards the door with his arm about his shoulder*): Yes, no doubt there will be a sensation, should I abandon you. You, my son-in-law, and I with the most abundant means at my disposal. And yet I did nothing, they will say. That will arouse their attention — they will become most attentive listeners. I need good listeners . . . and you will help me to get them. That will be your service. And praise shall be ours—even without my recognition. But my recognition will not fail.

45

(*The Officer goes out.*)

BILLIONAIRE'S SON *steps up to the table, passes his hand over the green cloth—nods—and then goes out behind to the left.*

The First Gentleman in Black enters from the left. A massive head with short bristles of grey hair rises above the closely-buttoned black frock-coat.

The Second Gentleman in Black enters—he is bald—and his costume, like that of all following him, resembles that of the First.

SECOND GENTLEMAN IN BLACK: How are things at your place?

FIRST GENTLEMAN IN BLACK: Not a finger moving.

SECOND GENTLEMAN IN BLACK: The same thing at my place.

(*Enter Third Gentleman in Black—with blonde pointed beard.*)

THIRD GENTLEMAN IN BLACK (*to the First*): How are things at your place?

FIRST GENTLEMAN IN BLACK: Not a finger moving.

THIRD GENTLEMAN IN BLACK (*to Second*): And with you?

SECOND GENTLEMAN IN BLACK *shakes his head.*

THIRD GENTLEMAN IN BLACK: The same with me.

46

(*The Fourth and the Fifth Gentleman in Black enter—two brothers closely resembling each other, about thirty.*)

FOURTH GENTLEMAN IN BLACK (*to the First*): How are things at your place?

FIFTH GENTLEMAN IN BLACK (*to Second*): How are things with you?

THIRD GENTLEMAN IN BLACK (*to both*): How are things with you?

FOURTH and FIFTH GENTLEMEN IN BLACK: Not a finger moving!

FIRST GENTLEMAN IN BLACK: The same with us.

SECOND GENTLEMAN IN BLACK: This is the most tremendous stoppage of work I have ever experienced.

FIFTH GENTLEMAN IN BLACK: And what is the cause?

THIRD GENTLEMAN IN BLACK: Our workmen are striking in sympathy with these men here.

FIFTH GENTLEMAN IN BLACK: Why are they striking?

SECOND GENTLEMAN IN BLACK: Because the Engineer has not been discharged.

FIFTH GENTLEMAN IN BLACK: Why is he kept on?

SECOND GENTLEMAN IN BLACK: Yes, why?

47

Fourth Gentleman in Black: Because of a mere whim!

Third Gentleman in Black: Just so!

First Gentleman in Black: There may be another reason. A reason based on principle. They demand the dismissal of the Engineer—that gives them something to fight about—furnishes a difficulty—a stumbling-block. If the workers make demands upon us—we must oppose these demands—unconditionally. That has been the case here—and, therefore, the Engineer keeps his post!

Third Gentleman in Black: But you forget that he is not one of us.

Fourth Gentleman in Black: It is another whim—of our friends—just like the first.

Second Gentleman in Black: And just as dangerous as the other. You will see!

Second Gentleman in Black: It is to be hoped that it is not more dangerous!

Third Gentleman in Black: I am of the opinion it could not be worse.

Second Gentleman in Black: This one affair causes us enough trouble!

Fourth Gentleman in Black: The whole body of workers has its eyes on these works!

Fifth Gentleman in Black: This sharing of

profits with everybody causes unrest in all the other syndicates.

SECOND GENTLEMAN IN BLACK: An ulcer which ought to be burnt out!

THIRD GENTLEMAN IN BLACK: With fire and brimstone!

FIRST GENTLEMAN IN BLACK: But you must not overlook the results which have been attained on the basis of this method. The sharing of profits has brought about the highest intensification of production, and this has brought about the most powerful of all products—Gas!

SECOND GENTLEMAN IN BLACK: Yes—Gas!

THIRD GENTLEMAN IN BLACK: Gas!

FIFTH GENTLEMAN IN BLACK: At any rate we need Gas.

FOURTH GENTLEMAN IN BLACK: Under all circumstances.

THIRD GENTLEMAN IN BLACK: We must present our demand: the dismissal of the Engineer.

SECOND GENTLEMAN IN BLACK: Quite independently of the workmen!

FIFTH GENTLEMAN IN BLACK: Quite independently of the workmen.

FOURTH GENTLEMAN IN BLACK: That saves our faces!

THIRD GENTLEMAN IN BLACK: Have you got the order of business?

FOURTH GENTLEMAN IN BLACK (*at the table*): Nothing on hand here.

FIRST GENTLEMAN IN BLACK: We have only this point to consider. Are we of one mind?

(*The other Gentlemen in Black shake his hand in agreement.*)

(*Enter the Son of the Billionaire from the left to the rear. He points to the chairs upon which the Gentlemen in Black quickly seat themselves. The Son of the Billionaire seats himself last, between the Fourth and Fifth Gentlemen in Black.*)

FIFTH GENTLEMAN IN BLACK: Who will take down the minutes?

BILLIONAIRE'S SON: No, no, let there be no minutes.

THIRD GENTLEMAN IN BLACK: A meeting and no minutes!

BILLIONAIRE'S SON: Yes, yes, we'll have an open discussion.

FIRST GENTLEMAN IN BLACK: Considering the importance of the matter I hold it as absolutely necessary that—in all cases our independence of a similar demand by the Workmen be——

SECOND GENTLEMAN IN BLACK: I move that the minutes of the meeting be published!

50

THIRD GENTLEMAN IN BLACK: Let us vote upon that.

FIRST GENTLEMAN IN BLACK: Those who are for——

(*The Gentlemen in Black each fling up an arm with a vigorous gesture.*)

BILLIONAIRE'S SON (*forcing down the arms of the Fourth and Fifth Gentlemen in Black*): Not all against one—that would make me too powerful. That would be coercing you—and I wish only to persuade you.

FIRST GENTLEMAN IN BLACK: If our negotiations——

BILLIONAIRE'S SON: Do you wish to negotiate with me? Are you the workmen? Are you not the masters? the employers?

THIRD GENTLEMAN IN BLACK: You have invited us without drawing up the order of business for the day. We conclude from this that you wish us to draw up this order ourselves. That, surely, is a just conclusion. We have agreed and are unanimous upon one point.

SECOND GENTLEMAN IN BLACK: I think the discussion will be brief, and that we had better return to our own plants.

FOURTH GENTLEMAN IN BLACK: It is high time that we begin work once more.

FIFTH GENTLEMAN IN BLACK: The first night-shift will begin work this evening.

THIRD GENTLEMAN IN BLACK: There are losses which can never be made good.

BILLIONAIRE'S SON: Losses? You have had losses? What have *you* lost?

THE GENTLEMEN IN BLACK (*together*): No work is going on—the plants are lying still—the workmen are on strike!

BILLIONAIRE'S SON (*lifting up a hand*): I know; they are holding funeral exercises. Surely they have good reason. Were not thousands—burnt?

FIRST GENTLEMAN IN BLACK: The strike is quite a different motive.

BILLIONAIRE'S SON: No, no! You must not listen to their speeches. These are senseless. What would you say when I tell you that they demand the dismissal of the Engineer? Isn't that a sign of their muddled minds? No, they do not know out there what they are doing.

THE GENTLEMEN IN BLACK *look at him in perplexity*.

BILLIONAIRE'S SON: Is the Engineer guilty, and must he do penance by resigning? Was his formula bad? It stood the test before—and it stands the test now. Upon what pretext could I send him away?

SECOND GENTLEMAN IN BLACK (*nodding*): The formula has been tested——

THIRD GENTLEMAN IN BLACK (*also nodding*): Its validity has been proved——

FOURTH GENTLEMAN IN BLACK (*also nodding*): It is the formula——

FIFTH GENTLEMAN IN BLACK (*also nodding*): For Gas!

BILLIONAIRE'S SON: Do you really realise this?

FIRST GENTLEMAN IN BLACK: And for that reason it may be applied by any Engineer.

SECOND GENTLEMAN IN BLACK: This or that one.

FOURTH GENTLEMAN IN BLACK: The Engineer is a mere side-issue.

FIFTH GENTLEMAN IN BLACK: A new Engineer —and the same old formula!

THIRD GENTLEMAN IN BLACK: And thereby the strike comes to an end.

FIRST GENTLEMAN IN BLACK: We are assembled here to present our demands—the dismissal of the Engineer!

BILLIONAIRE'S SON (*staring*):——Have you forgotten—are you still deaf—is the thunder and the crashing no longer rolling in your ears—are you no longer shaken upon your seats?—are you paralyzed?

53

SECOND GENTLEMAN IN BLACK: The catastrophe is a dark page——

FOURTH GENTLEMAN IN BLACK: We book it to profit and loss——

FIFTH GENTLEMAN IN BLACK: And turn over a new leaf!

BILLIONAIRE'S SON: The same formula!

FIRST GENTLEMAN IN BLACK: We hope——

SECOND GENTLEMAN IN BLACK: Naturally!

BILLIONAIRE'S SON: The same formula——?

THIRD GENTLEMAN IN BLACK: Perhaps there will be a longer interval between the——

FOURTH GENTLEMAN IN BLACK: One must gain experience!

BILLIONAIRE'S SON: Twice—thrice——?

FIFTH GENTLEMAN IN BLACK: We shall know when to expect the next——

SECOND GENTLEMAN IN BLACK: It is not likely that we shall live to see it.

BILLIONAIRE'S SON: I am to let them in—surrender——?

FIRST GENTLEMAN IN BLACK: After all, the industry of the entire world cannot be permitted to stand still.

THIRD GENTLEMAN IN BLACK: It is entirely dependent upon Gas!

BILLIONAIRE'S SON: Is it that? Am I the

source of energy which sets all this in motion?
Is my power as vast as that?

(*The Gentleman in Black regard him in amazement.*)

BILLIONAIRE'S SON: My voice is mighty—
mightier than horror and joy! Does the choice
between being and non-being depend upon my
word? Does the yes or the no which my lips
may speak determine Life—or Annihilation—?
(*Lifting his hands.*) I say—no!—no!—no! A
human being decides—as a human being only
can decide, no!—no!—no!

(*The Gentlemen in Black look at one another.*)

FOURTH GENTLEMAN IN BLACK: That——

FIFTH GENTLEMAN IN BLACK:——is——

THIRD GENTLEMAN IN BLACK:——really——

SECOND GENTLEMAN IN BLACK: What—is—
the——

BILLIONAIRE'S SON: The wreckage lies there—
and above the wreckage there is new soil—layer
upon layer—the growth of the earth in a new
garment—the eternal law of Becoming.

FIRST GENTLEMAN IN BLACK: What does this
mean?

BILLIONAIRE'S SON: Never again shall smoke-
stacks belch here! Never again shall machines
pound and hammer. Never again shall the cry

of the doomed be mingled with the—unavoid-able—Explosion.

SECOND GENTLEMAN IN BLACK: The plant——

THIRD GENTLEMAN IN BLACK: The recon-struction——

FIRST GENTLEMAN IN BLACK: Gas?

BILLIONAIRE'S SON: No reconstruction!—no plant!—no Gas! I will not take the responsi-bility upon myself—no man can take it upon himself!

FIRST GENTLEMAN IN BLACK: We are——

THIRD GENTLEMAN IN BLACK: —— to do without——

FIFTH GENTLEMAN IN BLACK:——Gas?

BILLIONAIRE'S SON: Without human sacrifices!

SECOND GENTLEMAN IN BLACK: We have established everything upon a basis——

THE OTHER GENTLEMAN IN BLACK:——of ! Gas

BILLIONAIRE'S SON: Invent a better Gas—or make shift with an inferior one!

FIRST GENTLEMAN IN BLACK: This is monstrous. We unqualifiedly reject all such imputations. What does it mean?—nothing less than a trans-formation of our entire plants——

FOURTH GENTLEMAN IN BLACK: The costs would be ruinous!

56

THIRD GENTLEMAN IN BLACK: It is not a matter of costs—even if these should bankrupt some of us. What I ask is this: shall the production of the world be reduced?

FIFTH GENTLEMAN IN BLACK: And that is why you must produce Gas. It is your duty. Now, if we had not had your Gas——

SECOND GENTLEMAN IN BLACK: You have brought about the highest development of modern mechanics. And now you must continue to supply Gas!

FIRST GENTLEMAN IN BLACK: By means of your advanced and fruitful methods which give your workmen a share in the profits, you have achieved this great finality—Gas. And that is why we tolerated this method—and now we demand Gas!

BILLIONAIRE'S SON: The method is indeed fruitful—as I have discovered. But I have merely gone these ways a little sooner than yourselves. Sometime or other you must all follow— the wages of all to be shared by all.

FIFTH GENTLEMAN IN BLACK: This formula should not have been invented—if there was any likelihood that the making of Gas was to be suspended sometime or other!

BILLIONAIRE'S SON: The invention was necessary—for the fever for work possessed the world. It raged blindly, and flooded all the frontiers of life.

FIRST GENTLEMAN IN BLACK: A reduction of the speed to which we have been accustomed could not be enforced.

BILLIONAIRE'S SON: No I do not councel a return to a feebler, slower movement. We must go on—leaving only the finished, perfect thing behind us—or we should be unworthy of our task. We must not succumb to cowardice. We are men— human beings imbued with a mighty courage. Have we not once more shown this courage? Did we not bravely exhaust every possibility?— It was only after we saw dead men by the thousands lying about us, that we struck out for new fields. Have we not once more tested the elements of our power and driven it to extremes merely to know how much power we enjoyed— to fetter the whole—to fetter mankind? Surely our pilgrimage goes towards mankind—epoch upon epoch—one epoch closes to-day so that the other may open—perhaps the last of all.

SECOND GENTLEMAN IN BLACK: . . . Do you really intend to stop all production?

BILLIONAIRE'S SON: Man is the measure for me—and the needs that uphold him.

58

THIRD GENTLEMAN IN BLACK: We have other needs.

BILLIONAIRE'S SON: As long as we exhaust man in other ways.

FOURTH GENTLEMAN IN BLACK: Do you wish to gull us?

FIFTH GENTLEMAN IN BLACK: With pamphlets?

BILLIONAIRE'S SON: I will set an example—establish it on my own land—there will be small domains for all of us in the midst of green promenades.

FIRST GENTLEMAN IN BLACK: What! you are going to cut up the most valuable tract of land in the world—for *such* a purpose!

BILLIONAIRE'S SON: The purpose—is Man!

THIRD GENTLEMAN IN BLACK: You must have command of great means, for the world takes account only of—money.

BILLIONAIRE'S SON: Our former profits will suffice for such a period as will be necessary before our new enterprise can take root and grow.

FOURTH GENTLEMAN IN BLACK: You would have to wait long before you found any imitators!

BILLIONAIRE'S SON: And what if there should be no Gas for you?

(*The Gentlemen in Black are silent.*)

BILLIONAIRE'S SON: I could force you—as you see—but I do not wish to force you. It would offend you—and I have need of your help. Here we are—six of us seated about this table—let us say the six of us get up and go forth, and our voices become a sextuple thunder which all men must hear. The dullest, deafest ear would hear our message, under this sixfold pressure. You are the great ones of the earth—Labour's Great Gentlemen in Black—arise and come forth and we shall proclaim that the fulness of time has fulfilled itself—and tell it again and again to them who will not understand, because the whirlwind which shook them until yesterday is still in their blood. Arise—go forth!!

FIRST GENTLEMAN IN BLACK (*after a pause, during which he looks about the table, exchanging glances*): Are we unanimous? (*The Gentlemen in Black fling up their right hands.*) We will set a time-limit—until this evening. If we are not informed by then that the Engineer has been dismissed, we shall apply to the Government. We bid you good-day.

(*The Gentlemen in Black go out.*)

BILLIONAIRE'S SON (*seated at the table, rubbing his hand slowly across the green cloth, murmuring*): No——no——no——no——no——!

(*Enter the Officer in extreme perturbation—from the left.*)

OFFICER (*unbuckling his sword and about to lay it on the table. But he halts, and feverishly buckles the sword on again*): I———cannot———do———it ———I———cannot! (*He draws a revolver, places it against his breast, stalks slowly out, step by step. As the door closes, a shot is heard.*)

BILLIONAIRE'S SON (*rising, staring towards the door*): The world is out of joint—let others force it back again!

FOURTH ACT

A great circular hall of concrete, the upper part vague and nebulous. From the cupola of this hall a cone of light from a hidden arc lamp falls through dusk and dust, a mysterious illumination.

In the centre, directly under this lamp, there is a steep, small, pulpit-like platform of iron, with two winding stairs.

Workmen are assembled, there are many women. Stillness reigns. The Speakers in alternation appear suddenly upon the platform, almost as from a trap-door.

VOICES (*rapidly swelling*): Who?
GIRL (*with upraised arms*): I!
    (*Stillness.*)
GIRL: I'll tell you of my brother!—I no longer knew I had a brother. Someone left the house in the morning and came home at night—and slept. Or he left the house at night and came back in the morning—and slept. One of his hands was large—the other small. The large

hand never slept. It kept making the same movement—day and night. This hand ate up his
body and sucked up all his strength. This hand
grew to be the whole man!—What was left of
my brother? My brother who used to play
beside me—who made sand-castles with his two
hands?—He plunged into work. And this work
needed only one hand—one hand that lifted and
depressed the lever—minute after minute—up
and down, to the very second! He never missed
a stroke—the lever was always true—always
exact. And he stood in front of it and served it
like a dead man. He never made a mistake—
never missed a count. His hand obeyed his head
and his head belonged to his hand!—And that
was all that was left of my brother!—Was this
really all that was left?—Then one day at noon—
It came! Rivers of fire shot out of every crack
and cranny! And the explosion ate up the hand
of my brother. And so my brother gave up his
all!—Is that too little?—Did my brother dicker
about the price when they hired his hand to lift
that lever? Did he not suppress all that had made
him my brother—and turned him into a mere
hand?—And did he not at last pay for his hand
too?—Is the pay too little—to ask for the
Engineer?—My brother is my voice—do not

work before the Engineer is forced to leave!—
Do not work—you hear my brother's voice!
(*Bending over towards them.*)

GIRL (*crowding up from below*): And it is *my*
brother's voice!

(*The Girl descends into the Crowd. Stillness.*)

VOICES (*swelling forth anew*): Who?

(*A Mother stands on the platform.*)

MOTHER: I!

(*Stillness.*)

MOTHER: A Mother's son was ground to
pieces by the Explosion! What is a Son? What
was it the fire killed? My son?—I did not know
my son any more—for I had buried him long ago
—the first morning that he went to the works.—
Are two eyes that had a fixed stare from looking
at the sight-tube—are they a son?—Where was
my child—that I had born with a mouth to laugh
—with limbs to play? My child—that threw its
arms about my neck and kissed me from behind?
My child?—I am a Mother, and know that what
is born in pain is lost in sorrow. I am a Mother
—I do not groan over this. I stifle the cry on
my lips—I choke it down. I am a Mother—I
do not strike—I do not accuse—not I—it is my
child that calls—here! I gave it birth—and now
it comes back into my womb—dead!—from

Mother to Mother! I have my son again! I feel his throbbing in my blood! I feel him tearing at my tongue—I feel him crying, crying: Mother! Where have you been so long? Mother! you were not by me—Mother! you left me alone so soon—Mother! you did not smash the sight-tube—and it was no longer than a finger and as thin as a fly's wing.—Why did he not crush it himself—one touch had done it.—Why was his will so weak—and all his strength gone into his staring eyes? Why did the flames put out his eyes? Why? Why? Must he do everything—and demand nothing? What does it all mean compared to his loss? Here, look! a Mother—and there, look! the Engineer!

(*Women crowd closely about the foot of the platform.*)

WOMEN: It is our son!

MOTHER: Mothers and Mothers and Mothers you!——sons cry out in you—do not strangle their cries; stay away from the works—stay away from the works—there is the Engineer.

WOMEN: Stay away from the works!

MOTHER (*descends from the platform and mingles with the Women*).

(*Stillness.*)

VOICES (*loudly*): Who?

WOMAN (*upon the platform*): I!
          (*Stillness.*)

WOMAN: We had our wedding—one day. A piano played—it was in the afternoon. Everybody danced about the rooms. A whole day was ours—morning—noon—and night. My man, my fine big man, was with me one whole day. One day from morning till night. His life lasted a whole day!—Is that too much? Because a day has morning—and noon—and evening? And the night? Is that too long for a man's life?— It is wonderfully long—twenty-four hours—and a wedding! A wedding and twenty-four hours— and a piano—and dancing—don't these make up a life? What does a man expect? To live *two* whole days? What a time!—an eternity! The sun would grow tired of shining upon him! We only get a wedding once—but the iron car rolls on for ever. Forwards and backwards—backwards—and forwards—and the man goes with it —always with it—because the man is part of the foot. Only his foot is important—his foot operates the block-switch—making the car go and halt—and the foot works, works almost without the man that travels with it. If only the foot were not so closely tied to the man! The man would have a chance to live—but his foot

pins him to the car which rolls back and rolls
forwards—day after day—with the man fastened
by the foot. But then the Explosion came!
Why was my husband burned alive? Why the
whole man? And not only the foot which was
the most important part of my man? Why must
my man be burnt, body and limbs, because of a
foot?—Because foot and body and limbs were all
part of him, because the foot will not work
without the man. The foot cannot work alone—
it needs my man.——Is this plant like my man—
who lived only one day—his wedding day—and
died a whole life long?—Are not old worn-out
pieces replaced with new?—and the works go on
as before?—Is not every man a mere part, inter-
changeable with other parts—and the works go
on?—Do not fight for the man at the lever—do
not fight for the man at the sight-tube—do not
fight for the man on the iron car—the Engineer
blocks the way—the Engineer blocks the way!

WOMEN (*about the platform*): Not for our men!

GIRLS: Not for our brothers!

MOTHERS: Not for our sons!

(*The Woman leaves the platform. The Workman
appears on the platform.*)

WORKMAN: Girls—I am your brother. I have
sworn it—and I am your brother. I have sworn

—and I am burned as he was burnt. I am lying under the ashes and dust—until you send me back to the lever—in place of your brother—who was blown up.—Here is his hand—broad and stiff, for gripping a jerking lever.—This hand has had its earnings—they lay in the hollow of it—and this hand carried them home. And this hand never counted the wages—there they lay in the drawer—and filled the boxes—and became worthless. What can a hand buy—now that this hand has lost its motive power—your brother? What can a hand wish—desire? A single hand—and all the savings in the box?—That hand has been paid for—but not your brother!—He has been burnt alive—and has, therefore, become alive—and now he is crying for his wages——: give us the Engineer—give us the Engineer!

WORKMEN (*around the platform*): We are your brothers!

(*The Workman descends among them.*)

WORKMAN (*already standing on the platform*): Mother—I am your son!—he has grown alive again—for the sake of his eyes—those eyes that stared so because of the sight-tube—he has grown alive again. Your son lives again—in me—breathing and speaking! Mother—I sacrificed myself for a sight-tube as long as a finger—

Mother—I gave myself for the sake of the sight-tube—-Mother—I died all over my whole body—and all that remained alive in me were my two eyes! I poured my wages upon the table before you—you did not catch the coin in your apron—it rolled upon the floor—Mother—you no longer bend down to pick it up! Do not pick it up—do not pile it into stacks—you cannot build a house for your son with such columns! He lives in a glass capsule, narrow and poisonous—in the sight-tube—Read the tables in the office and see if you can find the price of a Mother—for my blood and the blood of my Mother—for it was blood that these eyes drank at the sight-tube. Count up your earnings, the premiums, the profits we share—are they enough to pay for a Mother and a Mother's son? The eyes fixed upon the sight-tube brought their profit—but the son came out of it with empty hands. Ought he not charge Heaven and Earth with this great debt? Is he not willing to accept a mere trifle in payment for this debt? What is this worth in comparison with his sacrifice? The Engineer? Only the Engineer! and my eyes look past the Mother and stare at the sight-tube—only the Engineer—only the Engineer!

WORKMAN (*below the platform*): I am a son!

(Workman on platform decends among them.)

WORKMAN *(now on platform)*: Woman—your wedding-day will come once more! That day—with its morning, its noon and its evening will be yours once more! It will be *the* day—and all the other days that follow it will not seem like days at all. Your husband will go rolling back and forth again on the iron car—forwards and backwards—a man attached to a foot that operates a switch!—Why don't you laugh—you whose whole life is crammed into a single day!—a man and a woman with a whole day between them—is it not a waste of time while the iron car is whizzing to and fro?—Doesn't the dancing foot feel for the switch-block even in the dance?—Can the piano shut out the sound of the iron wheels grinding the tracks?—No, not a single day belongs to you—or to your man!—the iron car keeps rolling, and the foot controls it, and the beat of it holds the man. Can a drop out of a bucket grow into a river—can one day out of a thousand days make up a life? Do not be deceived by the profits: no real profits could be spent in one day!—You have your profits—but you do not live! What good to you are profits—profits made by the foot—profits which make a man poor in living?—You have lost time—and

so you have lost life—you have lost everything—
time and life—and you should spit upon these
gains which are worthless in the face of what you
have lost! Cry out your losses—fill your mouths
with fury and curses, cry out: We have lost time
and life—shout!—shout!—shout! Shout your
demand—shout your will—shout what you want
—shout if only to prove you have a voice—shout
merely to shout—the Engineer!

WORKMEN (*throughout the entire hall*): Shout!
shout!

(*The Workman leaves the platform.*)

WORKMAN (*on the platform*): Girls and Girls—
we promise you!—Women and Women—we
promise you!—Mothers and Mothers—we
promise you—not one of us will drive a spade
into the rubbish—not one of us will lay a brick
—not one of us drive home a rivet in steel—
Our resolve remains unshakable—the Works
will never go up—unless they give us a new
Engineer! Come and crowd this hall every day
—Brothers and brothers—Sons and sons—Husbands and husbands—each as determined as the
other—and let there be one unbendable will in
the assemblies—up with your right hands—
out with the oath—no Gas—if this Engineer
remains!

ALL MEN, ALL WOMEN: No Gas!—if this Engineer remains!

(*Workman leaves the platform.*)

STRANGE WORKMAN: Our resolutions tally with yours—I am sent here by the men of our plant—and the plant is standing still! We are waiting, we are with you—until you give us the word to take up work again. Count upon us—state your demands!

ALL MEN, ALL WOMEN: The Engineer!

(*Strange Workman leaves the platform. Another Strange Workman ascends it.*)

STRANGE WORKMAN: I am a stranger to you. I hail from a distant factory. I bring you this message—we have laid down our work because you are on strike. We are with you to the last. Hold out—stand firm—force your demands—for you speak in the name of all—you are responsible for all!

ALL MEN, ALL WOMEN: The Engineer!

(*Strange Workman leaves the platform.*)

WORKMAN (*on platform*): We shout, but our shouts do not cause this hall to explode. Our shouts go thundering into the vault up there and echo from blocks of concrete, but they do not go ringing out into the world.—Out! out of the hall!—make for the house—his house—thunder

your cries at him who still keeps on the Engineer!
—Form ranks!—march across the waste of ashes
—go look him out—he cannot hear us here—he
cannot hear us here!

ALL MEN, ALL WOMEN: On to the house!!—
he cannot hear us here!
(*The Crowd pushes tumultuously towards the doors.
A stormy babble of voices.*)

VOICE OF BILLIONAIRE'S SON: I hear you—
here!

(*A deathly silence.*)

VOICE OF BILLIONAIRE'S SON: I am here—in
this hall—I have heard you!
(*A buzzing and craning of necks among the crowd.*)

VOICE OF BILLIONAIRE'S SON: I will answer you
—here in this very hall!

(*Great excitement and movement.*)

VOICE OF BILLIONAIRE'S SON: You shall listen
to me now!

(*A path is cleared for him.*)

CLERK (*leaping upon the platform*): Don't let
him speak!—Don't let him come up!—Crowd
together—don't make room!—Run! run out of
the hall!—run to the works!—Run!—and clean
up the rubbish—put up the scaffolds—rebuild
the plant!—Don't listen to him!—Don't listen to
him—Don't listen to him! Run!—run!!—I'll

73

run ahead—back to my desk!—I must write—write!—write!

(Rushes off platform.)

BILLIONAIRE'S SON (*on platform*): I have been in the hall from the very beginning. You could not see me, because I shouted with you. Girl, I was a brother to you—Woman, I was a husband to you—Mother, I was a son to you. Every cry that passed your lips passed my own! And now I am here. Here I stand—stand above you—because I must state the final demand which you cannot state. You make a demand, but your demand is only a sand-grain of the mountain of demands you must make. You scream and scold about a trifle. What is the Engineer? What is he to you? What can he be to you—you who have come through the fiery furnace? What can he be to you who have passed through Annihilation? What can the Engineer be to you? It is only a cry of yours, a word that means nothing, an echoing word!—I know the Engineer is like a red rag to you—the sight of him brings back the Horror to you, the mere sight of him. The Engineer and the Explosion are one—the formula could not keep the Gas in check—this Engineer controlled this formula—and this formula brought on the Explosion. You think that you can put

74

out the Explosion only after you have chased away the Engineer. And that is why you cry out against him.—Do you not know that the formula tallies? That it tallies, that it is correct to the very limits of calculation? You know this —yet you cry out against the Engineer!

VOICES (*sullenly*): The Engineer!

BILLIONAIRE'S SON: Your cry comes from a deeper source! Your demand comprises much more than you demand! I urge you to demand more!

(*Silence.*)

BILLIONAIRE'S SON: What was there so terrible about the Explosion? What did it burn up— what did it rend apart? Did it go booming and hissing over one of you—one of you who was not already mutilated before the Explosion? Girl— your brother—was he whole?—Mother—your son, was he whole?—Woman—your man—was he whole? Was there a single man in all the works who was whole and sound? What havoc could the Explosion wreak upon you?—You who were shattered before the walls fell—you who were bleeding from many wounds before the crash came—you who were cripples—with one foot—with one hand—with two burning eyes in a dead skull—can the Engineer make this good?

75

Can any demand make this good again? I tell you—demand more!—demand more!

GIRLS, WOMEN, MOTHERS (*shrilly*): My brother!—my son!—my husband!

BILLIONAIRE'S SON: Brother and Brothers—Son and Sons—Man and Men—the call goes forth, the summons soars up from this hall—over the wreckage—over the avalanches that buried brother and brothers—son and sons—man and men—and it comes circling back into your hearts—demand to be yourselves!

(*Silence.*)

BILLIONAIRE'S SON: Demand!—and I will fulfill!—You are men—you represent Humanity—in the son, in the brother—in the husband! A thousand ties bind you to all about you. Now you are parts—each is a perfect unit in the great Commonwealth. The whole is like a body—a great, living body. Deliver yourselves from confusion—heal yourselves!—you that have been wounded—be human, human, human!

(*Silence.*)

BILLIONAIRE'S SON: Demand!—and I will fulfill! Brother—you are a man—you are Man. That hand of yours which clutched the lever shall cripple you no longer!—Son, you are a man—your eyes shall leave the sight-tube and gaze into

the blue distances! Husband, you are a man—
your day shall be the day of all the days you
shall live!

(*Silence.*)

BILLIONAIRE'S SON: Space is yours—and all
that life can give within this space—it is Earth—
it is your home. You are human beings in the
great house of Earth. Every wonder is known
to you—your will opens the way to all things!—
In you the heavens reflect themselves and the
surface of the Earth is covered with the garment
of many-coloured grasses—as with a flood. The
Day's work is great and full of gladness and full
of many new inventions. But you are not
inventions—you are perfected even now—complete—from this new beginning onward. You
have achieved a greater humanity—after this last
shift you are done with the task to which you
had been pledged!—You have completed the
shift, toiled to the very extreme—the dead have
sanctified the ground—you, that part of you, lies
buried!

(*Silence.*)

BILLIONAIRE'S SON: All that you demand—I
will grant—To-morrow you shall be free human
beings—in all their fulness and unity! Pastures
broad and green shall be your new domains.

The settlement shall cover the ashes and the wreckage which now cover the land. You are dismissed from bondage and from profit-making. You are settlers—with only simple needs and with the highest rewards—you are men—Men!

(Silence.)

BILLIONAIRE'S SON: Come out of the hall— come, walk upon the new homesteads—take measure of the land! No great effort is needed— but all creation waits—limitless—vast! Come out of the hall—come into the open!

(He leaves the platform.)

(Silence.)

(The Engineer stands upon the platform.)

A VOICE *(shrilly)*: The Engineer!

ENGINEER: I am here!—Listen to me: I will bow to your will—I will go. I will take upon me the great shame which will be branded upon my brow—if I should go. I will take upon me all the curses which go howling up against me— and my departure shall be the confession of my monstrous guilt. I will be guilty—as you wish! —I will go—so that you may return to the works!—The way is free—it leads back to the works!

BILLIONAIRE'S SON *(from below)*: Come out of the hall!—and build up the colony!

ENGINEER: Stay here!—stay here in this hall! —my voice is big enough for all of you—here you can hear me thunder!

BILLIONAIRE'S SON: Come out of the hall!

ENGINEER: Stay in the hall—refuse to be frauds!

(*Growls and murmurs.*)

BILLIONAIRE'S SON: Hatred is still at work here —outside the winds will sweep it away.

ENGINEER: You cheat the very shame with which you would scorch me. I am going—and you must go—back to work!

BILLIONAIRE'S SON: Fling open the doors— out!—into the daylight!

ENGINEER: You must go back to the works.— Do not pile fraud upon fraud—do not betray yourselves. Face the victory you have won— the victory that crowns you—Gas!—It is *your* work which creates these miracles in steel. Power, infinite power, throbs in the machines which you set going—Gas!—*You* give speed to the trains which go thundering your triumphs over bridges which *you* rivet. *You* launch leviathans upon the seas, and *you* divide the seas into tracks which *your* compasses decree! You build steep and trembling towers into the air which goes singing about the antennae from which the sparks speak

79

to all the world! *You* lift motors from the earth and these go howling through the air out of sheer fury against the annihilation of their weight! You who are by nature so defenceless that any animal may attack and destroy you—you who are vulnerable in every pore of your skin—you are the victors of the world!

(*Profound silence.*)

BILLIONAIRE'S SON (*at the foot of the platform, pointing at the Engineer*): He is once more showing you the pretty picture-book—of your childhood days. He would tempt you with memories. But you are no longer children—for *now* you have become adult!

ENGINEER: You are heroes in soot and sweat.— You are heroes at the lever—at the sight-tube— at the switch-block. You persist grandly, immovably, amidst the lashing of the pulleys and the thumping and thundering of the pistons!— And even the greatest ordeal of all cannot appal you for long—the Explosion!

BILLIONAIRE'S SON: Come out of the hall!

ENGINEER: Where would you go?—would you leave your kingdom and enter a sheepfold? Go pottering from early till late in the tiny quadrangle of your farms? Plant paltry weeds with those hands of yours—hands that created

towering forces? And your passion for work—
shall it serve merely to nourish you—and no
longer create?

BILLIONAIRE'S SON: Come out of the hall!

ENGINEER: Here you are rulers—in these
works where the motive power of the whole world
is born—you create Gas! There is your rule,
your mastery—the empire you have established—
shift upon shift—day and night—full of feverish
work! Would you barter this power for the
blade of grass that sprouts as it will?—Here you
are rulers—there you are—peasants!

A VOICE (*crying*): Peasants!

OTHER VOICES: Peasants!

MORE VOICES: Peasants!

ALL MEN, ALL WOMEN (*a torrent of shouts and
upflung fists*): Peasants!!!

ENGINEER *stands there in a triumphant attitude.*

BILLIONAIRE'S SON (*at foot of the platform*): Will
you listen to him—or to me?

ALL MEN, ALL WOMEN: To the Engineer!

ENGINEER: The Explosion has *not* sapped your
courage! Who gives in to Fear?

BILLIONAIRE'S SON: I do not wish you to fear.—
Is it not I who make the greater demands upon
your courage?—Do I not ask you to realise—
Man? How can you become peasants again—

after you have been workmen?—Do we not expect you to climb still higher? The peasant in you has been overcome—and now the Workman must be overcome—and Man must be the goal! This mission thrusts you forward—not backward. Have you not ripened—after this last experience? How far could you still go—working with your hands—working in shifts?—Are your thundering trains, and vaulting bridges and flying motors sufficient recompense for your fever? No, you would laugh at the miserable wages!—Are you tempted by the rich profits which we share? But you waste these again—as you waste yourselves!—The fever is in you—a madness of toil, which brings forth nothing. It is you that the fever eats. It is not your house that you build! You are not the wardens—you sit in the cells! You are pent about by walls, and these walls are the work of your own hands. Come forth! I say, come forth! You are heroes—who do not fear the new adventure! You do not fear to go to the end of the road—terror cannot palsy your steps! The road has come to an end—exalt your courage with fresh courage—Man has arrived!

ENGINEER: You would be peasants, slaves to grubbing toil!

BILLIONAIRE'S SON: You are men—in all your Wholeness and all your Oneness!

ENGINEER: Petty needs will mock your rightful claims!

BILLIONAIRE'S SON: All that you hope for you shall receive!

ENGINEER: Your days would be lost in sloth!

BILLIONAIRE'S SON: You are working at a time-less task!

ENGINEER: Not a single invention could take form!

BILLIONAIRE'S SON: You are honourably dis-charged—you are promoted—to human be——

ENGINEER (*holding a revolver over his head*): Shout—and let destruction come!

BILLIONAIRE'S SON: Leave destruction and come forth to the consummation—of Humanity!

ENGINEER: Shout!—and your shout shall destroy me—but go back to work!

(*The muzzle is at his temple.   Silence.*)

ENGINEER: Dare the word!

VOICE (*suddenly*): The Engineer shall lead us!

VOICES and VOICES: The Engineer shall lead us!

ALL MEN, ALL WOMEN: The Engineer shall lead us!

ENGINEER: Come out of the hall!!—back to

the works!—From Explosion to Explosion!!—Gas!!

ALL WOMEN, ALL MEN: Gas!

(*The Engineer leaves the platform. Broad doors are flung open. The Workers stream out.*)

BILLIONAIRE'S SON (*tottering upon the platform*): Do not strike down your brother Man! You shall not manufacture cripples! You, Brother, are more than a hand! You, Son, are more than a pair of eyes!—You, Husband, live longer than one day!—You are eternal creatures—and perfect from the very beginning!—do not let the days mutilate you, nor dumb mechanical movements of the hand—be greater, be greedy for the higher thing—in yourselves—in yourselves!!

(*Empty hall.*)

BILLIONAIRE'S SON (*summoning up all his strength*): I have seen man—I must protect him against himself!

FIFTH ACT

A wall of brick or concrete, partly shattered and b,*ackened by the Explosion. A wide iron gate, thrown from its hinges, in the centre of this wall. A waste of rubbish.*

Outside the gate a soldier with rifle and fixed bayonet.

The Billionaire's Son with a bandage about his head, standing in the shelter of the wall.

An Officer, a Captain, in a waiting attitude, in the centre.

BILLIONAIRE'S SON: It is all a horrible mistake. I must speak—I must explain.

CAPTAIN: They met you with a volley of stones.

BILLIONAIRE'S SON: They would not do it a second time—when they see that they have injured me.

CAPTAIN: I would not be so sure of that.

BILLIONAIRE'S SON: The sight of the soldiers angers them. That is the real reason.

85

CAPTAIN: You sought this shelter yourself.

BILLIONAIRE'S SON: Not for myself. I wanted to shut off the works. I could do that in three or four words.

CAPTAIN: They won't let you speak even one word.

BILLIONAIRE'S SON: But surely they would not attack me—when I want to justify myself!

CAPTAIN: Keep close to the wall!

BILLIONAIRE'S SON: Will you escort me out?

CAPTAIN: No.

BILLIONAIRE'S SON: No?

CAPTAIN: They might also attack me—and I would be obliged to open fire.

BILLIONAIRE'S SON: No, no, not that!—I must wait then, until they come to their senses !

(*The Soldier before the gate is relieved by another Soldier. Cries and clamour from thousands of throats.*)

BILLIONAIRE'S SON: What are they shouting for now?

CAPTAIN: The sentry is being relieved.

BILLIONAIRE'S SON: This confusion is terrible! Can't they understand what I am after? They are my brethren—I am merely older, more mature—and must keep my hand over them!

(*Enter the Government Commissioner from the right.*)

GOVERNMENT COMMISSIONER (*at the gate, peering out*): The situation looks serious! (*To the Captain*): Are you prepared for all emergencies?

CAPTAIN: Machine-guns.

(*The tumult without has arisen afresh and continues until the Government Commissioner moves away from the gate.*)

GOVERNMENT COMMISSIONER (*to Billionaire's Son, lifting his top-hat, and looking for papers in his portfolio*): The extraordinary and dangerous developments in your works have compelled the Government to discuss the situation with you. May I present my authorisation?

BILLIONAIRE'S SON (*taking the paper, reading, looking up*): Full powers?

GOVERNMENT COMMISSIONER: Under certain conditions. Shall we proceed to negotiations—here?

BILLIONAIRE'S SON: I shall not leave this place.

GOVERNMENT COMMISSIONER (*putting the paper back into his portfolio, taking out another*): The events which have led up to this strike may, no doubt, be summarized as follows:—After the catastrophe the workmen refused to take up the rebuilding of the plant because certain conditions which they had made were not accepted by you,

87

these conditions involving the discharge of the Engineer.

BILLIONAIRE'S SON: That would not have prevented fresh catastrophes!

GOVERNMENT COMMISSIONER: The Government can recognise only facts.

BILLIONAIRE'S SON: But the Explosion is certain to occur again—there is only this formula—only this—or no Gas!

GOVERNMENT COMMISSIONER: Future eventualities cannot be accepted as evidence. The condition imposed by the Workmen was rejected by you. As a consequence the Workmen continue the strike—which has now spread to neighbouring works, and is extending itself from day to day.

BILLIONAIRE'S SON: Yes. Yes!

GOVERNMENT COMMISSIONER: In the meantime the Engineer has offered his resignation at a meeting of the Workmen. A sudden change of feeling on the part of the Workmen induced them to drop their demand, and now they wish the Engineer to remain.

BILLIONAIRE'S SON: Yes!

GOVERNMENT COMMISSIONER: The cause of the strike has thereby been done away with, and the Workmen are willing to take up work again.

BILLIONAIRE'S SON: As you see—they are clamouring to get in.

GOVERNMENT COMMISSIONER: But now you have issued an order forbidding them to return. You declare that you could not possibly render yourself responsible for the production of Gas!

BILLIONAIRE'S SON: No—for the destruction of human life!

GOVERNMENT COMMISSIONER: The Government is fully cognisant of the uncommon severity of the misfortune which has regrettably taken place.

BILLIONAIRE'S SON: That says little.

GOVERNMENT COMMISSIONER: The number of victims has called forth the greatest sympathy. The Government is preparing a vote of condolence in Parliament. The Government is of the opinion that in making this proclamation in so conspicuous a place it has done full justice to you and to the Workmen.

BILLIONAIRE'S SON: Yes. The Government has no power beyond this. The rest will be my task.

GOVERNMENT COMMISSIONER: It is with the gravest concern that the Government has heard of your further intentions of permanently keeping the works from being rebuilt.

BILLIONAIRE'S SON: You must not doubt my powers—I will carry out my plans!

GOVERNMENT COMMISSIONER (*drawing forth a new paper*): A conference as to how this danger may best be averted has already taken place.

BILLIONAIRE'S SON: Give me a few soldiers—and give me a guarantee that I shall be heard—out there!

GOVERNMENT COMMISSIONER: The danger involved in a stoppage of the production of Gas has induced the Government to make you a confidential communication.

BILLIONAIRE'S SON (*staring at him*): You—demand—Gas!

GOVERNMENT COMMISSIONER: The whole armament industry is operating upon a basis of Gas. The lack of this motive-power would inflict great damage upon the manufacture of war material. And a war is imminent. Our programme of armaments cannot be carried out without this supply of energy. It is this solemn contingency which forces the Government to declare that it cannot any longer tolerate a delay in the delivery of Gas to the armament plants!

BILLIONAIRE'S SON: Am—I—not—my—own—master—on—my—own—ground?

GOVERNMENT COMMISSIONER: The Government is impelled by a sincere desire to come to an understanding with you. It is prepared to further the reconstruction by every means in its power. Towards this end it has ordered four hundred motor-lorries, with tools and workmen— they will be here in the course of the hour. The clearance of the wreckage can be taken in hand at once.

BILLIONAIRE'S SON:——To make weapons— to be used against human beings!

GOVERNMENT COMMISSIONER: I trust that you will treat my communication with the utmost secrecy.

BILLIONAIRE'S SON: I—I will bellow it out— I will look for confidants in every nook and corner!

GOVERNMENT COMMISSIONER: I can well understand your excitement. But the Government is face to face with a grim necessity.

BILLIONAIRE'S SON: Do not blaspheme! It is Man alone who is necessary!—Why must you inflict new wounds upon him—we find it so hard to cure the old!—Let me talk to them—I must go——

(*At the gate. He is greeted with howls.*)

CAPTAIN (*pulling him back*): You will unloose the storm!

BILLIONAIRE'S SON (*tottering against the wall*): ——Are we all mad?——

GOVERNMENT COMMISSIONER: It is important that the Government should know whether or not you intend to persist in your refusal to let the Workmen recommence work?

BILLIONAIRE'S SON: Now—more than ever, I regard it as my duty— to refuse.

GOVERNMENT COMMISSIONER: You persist in your former refusal?

BILLIONAIRE'S SON: As long as I can breathe and speak!

GOVERNMENT COMMISSIONER: I must then make use of the power imposed in me by the Government. In view of the danger which threatens the defence of the Realm, the Government is obliged to dispossess you of your works for the time being and to carry on the manufacture of Gas under Government control. The reconstruction of the works will take place at the expense of the Government and will be taken in hand at once. We trust that we may count upon your making no attempt at resistance. We should greatly regret being forced to adopt more rigorous measures against you!—-Captain, open the gates —I wish to communicate the essential points to the Workmen.

(*At the gate. A stormy tumult breaks loose.*)

CAPTAIN: Stand back!—stones!

GOVERNMENT COMMISSIONER (*retreating to the shelter of the wall*): This is incredible!

(*The uproar continues.*)

GOVERNMENT COMMISSIONER: These people simply hinder——

BILLIONAIRE'S SON: I do not fear them——

(*At the gate. The uproar at its maximum.*)

BILLIONAIRE'S SON *holds up his arms on high.*

(*The surge of the tumult draws nearer.*)

CAPTAIN (*shouting to the Government Commissioner*): They are coming!

(*Goes through the gate—issues orders towards the left. A machine-gun detachment comes and takes up position. The Captain stands, holding his naked sword over his head, prepared to give the signal.*)

(*Deep silence.*)

GOVERNMENT COMMISSIONER (*close to the Billionaire's Son*): Why won't you forestall this bloodshed?

BILLIONAIRE'S SON *stands as though stunned.*

GOVERNMENT COMMISSIONER: Here (*he hands him his white handkerchief*). They will understand this sign. Wave this white flag!

BILLIONAIRE'S SON *obeys mechanically.*

GOVERNMENT COMMISSIONER: You see—that

93

works! They are dropping their stones! (*To the Captain*): Throw the gates wide open! (*Soldiers throw open the gates.*) Withdraw the cordon! (*The Captain and the machine-gun detachment withdraw. To the Billionaire's Son*): I will go tell them at what point the lorries will deliver the tools. I'll lead the people there myself!

(*Goes through the gate. Soon after high, clear shouts and cheers are heard without—these grow rapidly fainter.*)

(*Silence.*)

BILLIONAIRE'S SON *sinks upon a heap of débris*).

(*Enter the Daughter—in black.*)

DAUGHTER *goes up to him—puts her arms about his shoulders.*

BILLIONAIRE'S SON *looks up in surprise.*

DAUGHTER: Do you not know me?

BILLIONAIRE'S SON: Daughter!—in black!

DAUGHTER: My husband is dead.

BILLIONAIRE'S SON: Have you come to reproach me —Will you, too, cast a stone upon me?

DAUGHTER (*shakes her head*): Are you all alone here?

BILLIONAIRE'S SON: Yes, I am alone at last— like all men who wish to give themselves to all men!

94

Daughter (*touching the bandage about his fore-head*): Did they strike you?

Billionaire's Son: They struck me—struck me, too. There are bolts that rebound and wound both—the archer and the target.

Daughter: Is all danger over?

Billionaire's Son: Are men born? Born of women—men who do not scream nor make horrible threats? Has Time lost count of itself—and thrust Mankind into the light? What does Man look like?

Daughter: Tell me!

Billionaire's Son: I have lost all memory of Man. What was he like? (*He takes her hands.*) Here are hands—and growing to these—(*taking her by the arms*)—are limbs, members—and the body unites them—parts that are active, parts of the whole, and all a part of life———!

Daughter: Tell me!

Billionaire's Son: The torrent rages too hideously—it overflows the banks. Cannot a dam be built which will hold in the flood? Cannot this raging be bounded, cannot it be used to water the barren places of the Earth and convert them into pastures of peaceful green? Is there no halting? (*He draws his Daughter close to him.*) Tell me, where can I find Man?

When will he make his appearance—when will
he announce his name—Man? When will he
understand himself? And plant the Tree of his
Knowledge of Himself? When will he rid
himself of the primal curse?—when will he re-
create the creation which he has ruined—Man?
—Was I not happy in having had a glimpse of
him and his coming?—Did I not behold him
clearly with all the symbols of his fullness of
power—silent, yet speaking the tongue that all
the world understands?—Man! Was Man not
close to me—Mankind? Can Man be extinguished—must he not come again and again—
now that at least one man has seen his face?
Must he not arrive—to-morrow or the day after
to-morrow—every day—every hour? Am I not
a witness for him—and for his lineage and his
advent.—Do I not know him—his bold, beautiful
face? Can I doubt any longer?

DAUGHTER (*sinking on her knees before him*): I
will give him birth.